The Big HUSTLE

By James Arceneaux Jr.

The Arceneaux Group®

TheArceneauxGroup@yahoo.com

Ordering information

ISBN: 978-0-985161873

For details contact James Arceneaux at the email address above

Individual Sales - TheAreceneauxgroup@yahoo.com

Printed in the U.S.A.

Cover design Butterfly Grafix

Cover Photo: Pamela Mougin

Executive Editor: Carla J. Kennedy

Technical Editor: Johnny Macknificent Mack

Contents

Bio of James Arceneaux Jr 4

PREFACE 10

INTRODUCTION 12

DEDICATION 24

A WELL-OILED MACHINE 28

THE MUSIC 36

THE MOVIES 40

SEX & VIOLENCE IN ENTERTAINMENT 46

THE NEWS MEDIA 54

CELEBRITIES 60

ATHLETES 64

MANAGERS 68

THE ARTIST 84

THE ATTORNEYS 90

AGENTS 96

PROTECT AGAINST THE BIG HUSTLE 100

MY FINAL THOUGHTS 110

Bio of James Arceneaux Jr

I grew up in Portland, Oregon where I attended Humboldt grade school, Martin Luther King Jr. grade school, Cleveland High School, and John Adams High School. If you look in the John Adams High School yearbook at the photo captioned "Most Likely to Succeed" my photo isn't there. Known for being a prankster and super social, I decided making friends and being the center of both conversation and controversy would be my claim to fame. My photo was more likely to be found under the caption "He Isn't Going to Make It." A week before graduating from high school I was short 2 credits, credits I was warned about 2 months before graduation but clearly ignored. The moniker "He Isn't Going to Make it" was just about to ring true until my concerned vice principal Miss June Key, a person who truly believed in me, was determined to get me out of high school on time. She found 2 credits from a summer course I had already completed and used the credits as course electives so I could graduate with the rest of my class.

I was relieved I was going to make it after all. And ironically, I found myself encouraging my peers to strive for success. My best friend Elroy Bell and I gave the commencement speech at the graduation ceremony! Can you believe that?

After high school, I attended junior college where I played football and worked on my grades. I transferred to the University of Oregon to play football and finish my studies, and upon graduation, I moved to Honolulu Hawaii where I began my love for the entertainment business. Shortly after arriving, I opened a recording studio and at the same time began a food, beverage, and entertainment publication that allowed me to become popular in the local entertainment scene. A talented local jazz singer in Hawaii who was connected to some of the most successful artists in the business introduced me to Anita Pointer of the R&B group The Pointer Sisters. If you don't know them, you should! Their entertainment career spans over four decades, winning three Grammy Awards in the 70s and 80s. Anita and I became good friends and I decided to move to Los Angeles and pursue being a music manager.

After a year or two in Los Angeles, Anita and I began a romantic relationship, and I began partnering with her management team to help make decisions regarding her career. She and I traveled the world together and I participated in the entertainment business on levels unimagined. It allowed me to meet people I would have never been able to sit in the same room with had it not been for her trust in me, and her generosity and kindness.

While working and traveling with her, I met 3 sitting U.S. Presidents, attended every major music event in the world at

6

least once, and met dignitaries of foreign countries. I played golf at just about every great golf destination and resort in the world. One of my favorites was in Cairo, Egypt next to the world famous Giza pyramids. While at a stopover in Korea on my way to the Johnnie Walker Classic in Thailand, I met Tiger Woods and his father Earl long before Tiger was a household name.

The most exciting time I had was the night I met Michael Jackson at the Mirage Hotel in Las Vegas and he watched the Siegfried and Roy show with Anita and I. Thank you Anita Pointer for showing me the world in a way I may have never known. May God continue to bless your life and the gift you have shared with us. You gave us an amazing career in music and songwriting and we will embrace you and your talent forever.

Other talented people I've worked for in entertainment include Eddie Murphy, Sugar Ray Leonard, Johnny Gill,

Charlie Wilson, New Edition, Chris Spencer, and many more. Today, I'm an entertainment consultant, author and public speaker; I conduct seminars for those who desire to enter the entertainment business, business management, and providing education on the effect this industry has on our youth and society. I've made it my personal responsibility to help people see the dangers, not of pure entertainment or the entertainment business, but of its presentation and how that presentation is packaged and delivered to us all. If you pay attention and understand the game, you may not get hustled by The Big Hustle!

For Booking and Information

Contact James Arceneaux at

TheArceneauxGroup@yahoo.com

PREFACE

This is a book about the entertainment business. It's not a tell-all book about the lifestyles of the rich and famous and how dysfunctional they are. Truthfully, we're all dysfunctional, they just have their dysfunction displayed and criticized in public view. This is a tell-the-truth book about how the machine of entertainment is *The Big Hustle*. This business touches every aspect of our lives - TV, movies, professional sports, video games, children's movies, toys, politics, the news and even religion.

Not only will this book tell the truth about entertainment, hopefully some of the information shared will help those of you who are artistic navigate your way through the madness. It's a cautionary tool that can protect you from being hustled, and a host of horrible things that you have no clue are interwoven into every facet of this business.

The number of those who succeed in entertainment and make a good living are few, but the scars they received for their efforts in hindsight may not have been worth it. For you fans or casual spectators that consume entertainment every day, I'll share the subliminal effect it has on you, your family and your entire surroundings.

I remember reading a quote in an entertainment industry book that said "No matter how much you love this business it was never designed to love you back." How frightening is that? It's automated. It's calculated. It's a machine. It doesn't show human emotions nor care for you. It operates in a cybernetic manner which means you have real live people being controlled through virtual reality.

The entertainment industry is the manufacturer of fantasy at the highest level, a level so high it seems unfathomable. While it appears an attractive platform to display your talents, it will change *you* before you change it, and the only thing it cares about is getting you in and getting you in deep.

INTRODUCTION

I hope by the time you reach the last chapter, My Final Thoughts, you will have shared a journey with me through the entertainment business of today. A journey that will show you what the business is, what it does for you and to you, and who is affected by its agenda. The allure of the entertainment business has always been its ability to show you fantasy and then make that fantasy come to life - in other words, make you believe it. If you've ever listened to music, it got you; if you've ever watched television or a movie, it got you; if you've ever engaged in any form of entertainment, it got you.

It has captured all of us. I remember back in 1974 watching a documentary film in high school called *Subliminal Seduction* by Wilson Bryan Key. He shared the process of *subliminal advertising*, the way the industry uses film to arouse our desires to get us to do things we don't want to, and buy things we don't need. To this day, I've never forgotten that documentary because of how I've watched it play out in my professional and personal experiences. It seemed so farfetched back then, but here we are today with human behavior still being manipulated by the entertainment industry. Back in that time, they actually had a term to describe what subliminal seduction is. It's called "media rape," a term that infers someone is forceful in their attempt to get you to watch or participate in something that you may not agree with.

Things are no different now than back then. It's very easy to manipulate people because we are so caught up in our own personal lives we haven't the time to pay any attention to what inevitably will happen to us all if we don't monitor the way we consume entertainment. This isn't a forecast of the future nor a prophecy. It is just good old fashioned truth that we should feel obligated to give some attention to if you don't want to continue to be fooled. It has and will continue to affect all of us. I'm just beginning to understand how it's been affecting me my entire life.

My first memory of falling in love with music was in the 8th grade. I remember using a portable transistor radio. You could hear 4 or 5 stations clearly and the other stations you had to listen to through static. I lived in a town that had no R&B radio stations, so hearing an occasional R&B song was a treat. A R&B song would play on the radio maybe once or twice every hour. I would go to bed at night with a flashlight and my radio waiting for my favorite songs to play. I knew them all and the time they would play because songs back then would come on around the same time every night for a least a few weeks. Because we didn't live in what was called a soul or black music market, we only heard the top R&B singers of the time like James Brown, Marvin Gaye, The Temptations, The Four Tops, The Spinners, Diana Ross, Al Green, Gladys

Knight and the Pips, Earth Wind and Fire, Stevie Wonder and of course Michael Jackson and The Jackson 5.

Also during that time there was a show that would come on every Saturday morning called Soul Train. Soul Train allowed us to see these great singers on TV performing the songs we fell in love with. These were my only connections to the music I loved. One morning I distinctly remember watching Soul Train and saying to myself *Man those people are having fun. California has got to be the greatest place on earth, and one day when I get some money I'm going there.* Well I guess you can say I brought that vision into reality in a way I never planned or thought possible back at that age.

My enchantment of music continued throughout my childhood. One of the most memorable experiences of my life was when The Jackson 5 came to my hometown of Portland, Oregon. They were the opening act for Diana Ross. Toward the end of the performance they called a couple of the audience members on stage to dance with The Jackson 5. I was so excited and nervous at the same time. When I got on stage, I nearly fainted from standing that close to Michael Jackson. It was surreal and so emotional for me that I cried all the way back to my seat. Of course, the next day at school I was a local celebrity. There are people in my hometown today that remember that concert and remind me of that memory when I travel back home.

I recall times my parents would throw adult parties and we as kids would be their entertainment. We would be asked to dance for the guests and told that if we did, we'd get some money. I would perform as James Brown and my sisters would be my dancers, and we would be working it! I would use a kitchen broom as my mic and rip it up. I loved entertaining them! Back then I could do James Brown's famous camel walk, the splits, hit the ground and get back up, and if you couldn't bounce back up after the splits it wasn't the splits.

Major moments in my life were always associated with music or influenced by the music of that era. I remember being alone with a girl in the basement of our house in 8th grade trying to get her to like me. I was trying to figure out what I was going to say to her and I suddenly remembered lyrics to a song called "Love on a Two-Way Street" by The Moments, and I started reciting them to her. She was captivated by my words and believed me when I said I wrote them just for her. Even at that age, music was influencing my life and my actions in every way it could.

Another example of music's seduction on me growing up was a story my family still jokes about today. Being the only boy in my family growing up with sisters always around you, the only pastimes were to braid hair, play with dolls, play records, play jacks, talk about boys; or my preference of looking for trouble or playing football. Thank God for trouble and football! One evening my mother and father went out to dinner and left me home to babysit my younger sister. Well it also happened to be the night Earth, Wind and Fire was performing in Portland, and I was determined to go. I heard their show was off the chain and the hottest live performance show. A friend called and said he had tickets to the show for both of us. When I told him I couldn't because I had to babysit my sister, he replied "Man, you CANT miss this show! She'll be fine if you put her to sleep first." He was right! There was no way I could miss this show. His idea sounded like a good one to me. I told him I'd meet him there and left my 9-year-old sister at home alone.

I'm at the concert mesmerized by Earth, Wind and Fire's performance when a friend said to me "Somebody said your mom is in here looking for you and she looks real upset." I started thinking of a plan and decided I needed to get home

18

before she returned back there. My mind was racing as I exited the venue. I remembered a busy street I lived off that ran from the concert venue straight back to my house. I was pretty confident I could beat her home. I got a little tired of running so I decided to hitch hike, which was common to do at that time. I put my thumb up and waited for a car to give me a ride. After a few minutes, I saw a car slow down and pull up to me. I breathed a sigh of relief knowing I would certainly make it home before my mother now. I was so anxious to get in the car I didn't realize the car I jumped into was my parent's car! I assure you my mother is the sweetest woman in the world but that night the words she said to me will never be forgotten and still ring in my head today: *Fool, get your ass in this car! Have you lost your mind? I'm gonna beat the living daylight out of you. You left my baby at home by herself?! I'm gonna kill you when we get home. Boy, you must be under some kind of spell or something!* Little did she know how prophetic her words were.

My love for music elevated when I headed off to college to play football. I remember sitting on a greyhound bus with my cassette player and more batteries than I could count so that I could listen to music every second of my ride there. When I arrived on campus to play football, I didn't even look at my playbook. I set up my dorm room with my stereo, ready to usher me into college life. The music of The Commodores, Earth Wind and Fire, Natalie Cole, and many others were a staple throughout my college years. From there until today, I've had an unbelievable love for music, and it will always be my first entertainment love. For me, it just wouldn't go away. Music alone as a form of entertainment is tied to many defining moments in our lives.

I share these stories not just to tell you about the joy I experienced growing up with music in my life but also its effect on my life. I want to give you a glimpse into my journey. While I have this passionate love for music, I also recognize its attraction and seduction on those who lack awareness. If not monitored and controlled properly, it can become more than a seduction. My mother would say it's a spell that captivates your spirit.

My life is a script I could have never written. I've attended star-studded events where the guest list was the who's who of entertainment. I've traveled the world in private jets and worked for celebrities who are bigger than life, and yet I remain grateful and humble for those opportunities and special memories.

I've never used illegal drugs nor drank alcohol throughout my professional career in the entertainment business, so I have always been sober-minded and very aware of the environment I was in. When I told friends I was writing a book to share how this business works and entertainment's impact on our culture, their initial response was that I would tell stories of the private lives of those celebrities I've worked for over the past 25 years. No, that's not this book and I would never write that book. Most of the people I've had the opportunity and pleasure to work for and spend time with I would consider as my friends. And those who I'm not as close with today, I would still never violate their trust and confidentiality. Entertainers, like everyone else, deserve privacy and to be respected by the people they've hired or befriended and allowed into their homes and around their families.

Although it has been a nostalgic ride sharing stories about music and entertainment, I must still reiterate that this business of entertainment as a whole has an effect on us all. It's an effect that infiltrate our minds as we consume it on a daily basis. I assure you as much as I love it, I recognize it for what it is, how it can mesmerize, create fantasy and change who you are, because the bottom line is that it's a big hustle –

THE Big Hustle. And if you don't equip yourself with the knowledge and insight that I share in this book, the entertainment industry will hustle YOU.

I hope the information in this book challenges you to think about entertainment and its impact on every aspect of society. Do the research. If you discover that what I've shared with you is true, you have a decision to accept it or not. I've given you the response from my research, personal industry business experience and my life in the entertainment world. My hope is that you do not make the mistakes and pitfalls of so many others.

DEDICATION

This book is lovingly dedicated to all those who gave us entertainment as an expression of art from their hearts with no other motive other than to give us an opportunity to see things, feel things and give life as we know it a picture. And for those who have taken advantage of artists and their craft, and have used them for their money, may God forgive them for they haven't a clue what they've done. To all the amazing and talented people I've met in my journey through entertainment, may your gifts and talents be something that one day you can stand before your Creator and say to him "I've done what you've asked with what you gave me, thank you for the opportunity of allowing me to be an expression of you."

A special thanks to family, friends and to those who supported me and this project I say to you, God knows who you are and what you've done and will reward you accordingly. A very special thanks to Pamela Mougin for an amazing cover photo.

Anyone that's ever worked on a project of any significance knows that it takes more than one person to bring it to completion. If you're as fortunate as I've been, you'll have someone work on your project with the same care, heart, desire and vision as you. Carla Kennedy this is you. You've mesmerized me and others with your love, wisdom, work ethic, professionalism, attention to detail, godliness and belief in this project. I know personally that this book would have never been the book that it is had it not had your editing signature. The work you've done is at such a level I had to ask God to pay my debt to you because what you deserve for your work on this project is a price I can't pay. Thank you, Carla. I love you so much and I want you to know that your work has also become the heartbeat of this book, and because of that I'll be forever indebted to you.

I pray that the information in this book will equip you with the insight and understanding to know that just because something looks good and feels good doesn't always mean that it is good. The entertainment business is what it says it is - a business that entertains and that is all it does, don't ever forget that. So, whenever you feel your excitability beginning to override your sensibility, you'll know entertainment is lurking somewhere in the picture.

James

Λ

A WELL-OILED MACHINE

The entertainment industry has a seductive effect and amazing influence on all people across the globe. The engine that is the entertainment industry uses movie stars, musicians, athletes, models, politicians and even religious leaders to hustle their agenda to the mainstream. They are programing us to respond to the information they put out and to take action. The things we're being asked to ingest from this well-oiled machine are absolutely astonishing, yet we take it all in every day allowing it to stimulate our senses. And those things that are sexual and violent in its presentation appear to stand out the most.

Most of what is produced and delivered by the entertainment industry is unsuitable for our young people. Technology is growing at a pace faster than anything we've ever seen in previous decades, and many of us already believe we're headed to a place the human mind isn't prepared to comprehend. The entertainment business has stolen the attention of our youth, reducing the time they spend with family, friends, school, outdoor activities, and a chance to develop their own ideas and thoughts. Time that if used wisely could stimulate the mind and develop their character. All fields of entertainment today teaches our youth to be selfish, violent, and sexual. It also teaches them that they deserve to *win* instead of experiencing the results of teamwork and collaboration, and building a strong work ethic.

In 2002, the US Department of Commerce published that families who have children are 87% likely to have high internet usage in their homes, and that 90% of all elementary schools in America have access to the internet. This means our kids have access to the internet 10-13 hours a day while they're awake. And if that time is not properly monitored it will become a more serious problem than it already is. Not only are our youth seduced by entertainment online, they are being bullied by it.

The library, a place that was once used for resource, learning, and fostering academic achievement has been replaced by the world's newest and greatest source of information - the internet.

Years ago, I worked at the Michael Jordan summer basketball camp for kids, and during camp breaks we would have a sports quiz. I discovered some of the kids cheating by using their cell phones to search for the answers. I was disappointed that those kids didn't realize the purpose of the quizzes was to stimulate their minds and knowledge of the sport, and sadly, they only cheated themselves out of an opportunity to grow, and learn to play honest and fair. Not having those experiences and learning vital lessons as adolescents I believe contribute to misguided youth becoming misguided adults.

Many don't realize that the internet has potential for more abuse than anything they will ever encounter in their lifetime. If not monitored and controlled, young people can come upon all types of things that can be a detriment to their development and behavior. One of the biggest problems is access to sex websites that only require kids to misrepresent their age. The entertainment industry plays a dangerous game. It captures our children's minds and keeps us occupied as well. It influences our actions, our dress and physical appearance, and nicely packages all our desires. It's almost as if we are all under this profound spell - and we are. The price of our ignorance and lack of vigilance with ourselves and our youth is too high a stake to ignore.

The entertainment industry juggernaut is simply a Big Hustle, a well-oiled machine that has silently become the master of mankind. Without our consent or knowledge, it has become our voice. The best analogy I can compare it to is the pimp, prostitute and john relationship. The entertainment business is the pimp; artists, athletes and entertainers are the prostitutes; and the consumers are the johns. Believe it or not, we are all being pimped by this well-oiled machine that seeks to control our mind, body and yes, even our spirit.

In The Big Hustle, I share with you what the entertainment business is, what it's not, and how to protect yourself. You will hear how to avoid some of the pitfalls the business will seduce you into without you even knowing it. It exploits, manipulates, cheats, lies, steals, and overpowers those who refuse to put their guard up. And this my friends is the way it is. It will never change, it can't change, and it's too big of a machine to be stopped. However, I'd like to show you how this business disguises itself, and connect the dots to how all of this *hustling* is part of a plan bigger than you could fathom.

Music, television, movies, professional sports, gambling, politics and even religion are all under the spell of this massive machine.

Each entity mentioned is connected with or infused with some aspect of entertainment. No one is excluded, everyone is involved whether you acknowledge it or not. Over the years, we've all allowed the seduction and its manipulation to take place. When I think about this business, I'm reminded of Proverbs 6:27 in the Bible that says *Can a man put fire into his lap and not be burned?* The answer is absolutely not! Solomon, the writer of this proverb was saying that it is impossible to get out of certain situations if you allow yourself to become hypnotized by it. The books, movies, magazines, and music that entertainment provides us makes us ignorant to the penalties of what we're inadvertently involved in and consuming.

The plan the entertainment industry has for you is in full effect. Starting today look around and ask yourself: Do I live a complete contradiction of how I say I want to live my life? Could there be an agenda going on and is entertainment media influencing me and my family? Does entertainment really control everyone and everything? After reading The Big Hustle, I challenge you to do your own homework and evaluate for yourself. You'll be glad you did.

THE MUSIC

Music has played a pivotal role in entertainment's manipulation process. What makes music so dangerous is that it is designed to be repetitive. You play a song over and over and over again. Rap, pop, rock and roll, heavy metal and even today's modern gospel music plays a role in the manipulation of millions of people and their perception of today's culture.

Music crosses more lines than any art form in the history of entertainment. Music influences the way people eat, drink, sleep and think. You can listen to music anywhere, with or without others, it's always available. The lyrical content of music today has become so absurd and offensive. I'm surprised that some types of music haven't been banned all together, with as much crime and societal woes we have experienced where music was identified as influencing the young mind. Yet those who appear to be decent parents continue to allow their children to listen to this kind of music with no regard for the lyrical content's influence, and naively assume there will be no backlash from it. How ignorant can those parents really be?

Researchers for years have warned us about allowing our children to listen to music with dangerous lyrics. They've said that the effect popular music has on the behavior of our young people should be of serious concern. Lyrics about sex, drugs, violence, anger, depression, hatred and fantasy have become way more explicit and commonplace in our culture than ever before.

An analyst who works with the National Institute on Media said that of the top 10 artists in popular music, at least one song on their CD is a song with sex or violence in it. Music such as heavy metal, rap, rock, and reggaetón have been found to revolve around subject matters like sexual promiscuity, suicide, death, homicide, depression, violence, substance abuse, racism, liquor, homophobia, and hatred toward religion and women.

Have you observed the sexual behavior patterns of young people lately? Many of them listen to songs with degrading sexual content, and in return they act out in risker sexual behavior that can often lead to unwanted pregnancies, STDs and other emotional and developmental problems now and later in life. Degrading lyrics tend to objectify both genders, portraying men as sexual animals and women as only sexual objects. The long-term effect of music (along with other entertainment-centered influences like movies and social media) is that as our youth grow up with that exposure, the behaviors that follow becomes part of the fabric of marriage, family, raising children and part of larger societal problems. There is no sure fix, but we can monitor the situation better than we do today. All it takes is a little truth, honesty and awareness.

Most of us wouldn't entertain conversations that support or promote these subjects but we sure love to listen to their promotion, and let our kids hear it in the form of music over and over and over again. What in the hell is wrong with us? I take just as much responsibility as anyone. We all have sat idle and watched how music as entertainment has influenced, and in some cases destroyed our youth in today's culture.

We are such cowards. We claim to be the toughest nation on the planet and yet we allow this to happen to our children without a word, that's not tough at all it's actually a pretty weak position. I've taken a stand to speak up and educate the public who may be unaware of the music industry's influence. I've made it my mission to inform them that they do have a choice in the matter. What stand will you take?

THE MOVIES

Ah the movies. A great American pastime for decades. Movies influence our lifestyles in a way that captures your imagination. Where music and other types of entertainment only give you a glimpse of the picture, movies take you for the full ride. The goal of a film is to woo you with such fantasy that you want to jump into the picture and become a participant instead of a spectator, therefore making the scenario as real to life as possible. With technology advancing the capability and consumability of entertainment, I believe the envelope will be pushed even further for more fantasy-type realism.

The entertainment business wants to create a dependency on entertainment, to be your drug of choice. It wants to be the only thing you get high on, so they embody the role of a pimp and their prostitutes sell you their entertainment products for your consumption. The compelling and moral principle is that the entertainment business has already concluded that the masses are too stupid to be able to see what is going on and to think for themselves. Truthfully, that's a pretty accurate assumption.

The problem is that real life issues need human reasoning, something a computer will never be able to do. Technology has no sense of reasoning and only does what it is programmed to do. Thus, what you receive from technology is controlled by the "programmer." The entertainment machine is programmatically designed to distract you, seduce you and make you more dysfunctional than you already are. Then they make you feel like you're out of order so they can put you back in order their way.

This business wants our trust so that we give them the hearts and minds of our children to be guided and directed by the entertainment they have designed and programmed. This is what we're really dealing with. Most of us would view the children's movie business as family-friendly, ethical and moral, an institution you can trust. We've been taught to believe that the businesses that caters to children would never do anything to hurt, harm or offend them. I'd like to believe that but I've discovered too many things that are in direct opposition to that thought process. We must ask ourselves who runs these businesses and what is their personal and professional track record in demonstrating a level of care and consideration for what children are exposed to. Let's not forget that the intent of entertainment companies is not to be the moral compass for families.

This machine is designed to produce revenue, not to demonstrate good or moral behavior for your family. It has never been and never will be concerned about the collateral damage that any merchandise produced has caused. There is significant evidence that child-oriented movies have become more violent and more sexual in content over the past 20 years. Parents must be more careful than they are today of allowing children to watch these movies. Most of them have subliminal sexual messages that if you are not specifically informed of and shown these incidents blended into the film, you might not have ever seen them on your own. This is intentional. Movies are designed to influence us all. It is hard to avoid this if you do watch films and movies, but you do your own research and begin to sensor and monitor it for you and your family.

Madonna and a few other celebrities have said publicly that they won't allow their children to watch television. Madonna has said there is too much garbage on. Well no kidding. Steve Jobs was quoted as saying his children don't even have iPads. I wonder what that's all about? Maybe he knows something you don't about this entertainment technology tool? Why aren't we all picking up on these things? Maybe we don't want to, and that, my friends, is what I call being captured by The Big Hustle.

SEX & VIOLENCE IN

ENTERTAINMENT

Sex and violence is not only the theme of entertainment, it's the agenda. Society has convinced our youth that sex is casual and consequence free. That couldn't be a bigger lie, and we as adults with children know this. Once again, we're hustling one another. The oversaturated amount of sex and violence in TV, movies, music, and video games has had a host of negative effects not only on our thoughts but in our actions. The video game industry has captured the minds and imagination of young people in a terrible way. Are there any good video games for young people? Maybe, but the majority of them are not. Some of those games are the causes of violent behavior patterns in youth, and there is research to support this.

Video games often promote sex, violence and reckless behavior that affects families, the educational system, and effect our society as a whole, yet we continue to expose our children and ourselves to it. Stories of violence, sex crimes, and behavioral issues are reported daily on the news, radio, in newspapers and on the internet. The media shows us these stories and images because they have programmed us to love it and to be mesmerized by it, like when we drive past a car accident on the highway.

We've gotten so used to hearing about sex, crime and violent behavior that we are desensitized to it. Somehow, we keep getting a little too comfortable and forget what the agenda is and who's pushing the buttons. We must continually remind ourselves that this is *The Big Hustle*, and that communication media is still pure entertainment that functions as a connector between people in society and their issues.

Parents, civic leaders, religious leaders, teachers, community leaders, mental health experts, and a few politicians (those not on entertainment's payroll) would all agree that music, television, film, pro sports and video games all affect the psyche, how we think, and behavior of all people in general, but impact young people so much more. It's a shame, however, that these leaders who claim to care about society know this valuable information and are doing very little about it. This should be concerning to you that they are not taking action and sharing the message about entertainment's impact to any and every one who will listen. It took a while but I finally realized that the program of entertainment is so powerful, it's even infected the people that are supposed to help us be free from its seduction, control and influence, including myself.

Since realizing this, I'm making efforts, outside of the knowledge shared in this book, to help rectify the problem and be part of the solution. I want to equip the masses with the knowledge to become more aware of how gravely they are being affected by the entertainment machine. My fear is that things will continue to go in a circle until something is done at a higher level. How severe does it have to get before we change the way we perceive entertainment's impression on us? I must reiterate that not all entertainers are bad, but the entertainment industry is infected with a disease that has been successful in its design to seduce, manipulate and control the people, and the amount of medicine needed to cure it we may not have.

Hollywood keeps telling us there is no connection between the entertainment we consume and people's behavior, and we either keep believing them or we are just too afraid to tell them they're liars. Have you noticed in the word *believing* is also the word *lie*? Now you know how the subliminal part of this works. Maybe we just need to experience a few more significant events in this country to jolt us off our asses and begin to protect ourselves and our most valuable treasure, our young people.

Law officials remind us daily that entertainment influences people far more than we'll ever realize. They have stated that many murderers have been found to have child pornography in their possession when arrested. For years, the law enforcement community has said that there is a direct relationship between vicarious violence and real violence. Those who produce films that glamorize violence are rarely willing to admit to the fact that a mind which feeds on violence from movies, TV, film, music and video games is more likely to react violently in real-life situations. Please remember that the entertainment business is not in the emotional or mental health business, nor are they babysitters, nor will they properly address all the evidence of their detriment to our society. It would cost too much to make it right. They're in business to make a profit off of entertaining us, regardless of the outcome. Compare this to the tobacco industry who knew the dangerous effects of smoking but marketed to the masses for decades, hiding the real effects from consumers. Executives and those in power on every level of the box office business just aren't concerned with collateral damage. They have one agenda, one big hustle, and that is to manipulate you to do what they desire. They do not take responsibility for promoting morality or good conduct just because you consume or buy an entertainment product. Their disclaimer is *get involved at your own risk.* They warned us, so now the ball is in our court.

As a nation, we say we are "under God." Well, we used to. Regardless, if we really were, here's what God says, *"The way of peace they know not; and there is no judgement in their goings; they have made crooked paths; whosoever goeth therein shall not know peace.* (Isaiah 59:8 KJV). This describes the directionless living that is present in our society. Most people are wondering around being led by whatever makes them feel good. The entertainment business knows this and takes full advantage of that opportunity, thus leading the consumer into the next big hustle.

THE NEWS MEDIA

For some strange reason the word *choice* in America always seems to be attached to something that restricts that choice. We have always had a restrictive type of liberty. Choice in America is an illusion when it comes to news media. I often laugh when my friends tell me they don't watch or listen to certain news channels because they don't like the reporter, what they are saying or the program. I laugh because they aren't aware that most of the news media is connected under the same ownership, and at the end of the day their agendas are all the same. This may come as a surprise to many of you but there are only six corporations that own all major news sources in America: General Electric, Disney, CBS, Viacom, Time Warner and News Corp. These are the big hustlers that control news media.

If you thought you had more choices, welcome to the real world. Media in America has never been more consolidated than it is today. As a matter of fact, the entire world is more consolidated today than it has ever been in the history of mankind, mostly because of the internet.

Two hundred and thirty two executives control the information diet of 277 million Americans. That would be one executive per 850,000 people in America, and total revenue for these six corporate giants back in 2010 was $275.9 billion dollars. Here are some ideas of what you could do with that kind of money. You could buy every team in the NFL 12 times over, and you could bail out General Motors five times. Hard to fathom, isn't it? These six corporate hustlers also control 70% of cable television in America.

Here are some other interesting facts about their hustle: the Comcast/NBC merger allowed them to control 1 out of every 5 hours of television daily. News Corp owns the top 3 newspapers on 3 continents, and in 2010 they avoided $875 million in US taxes. And you're worried about Donald Trump and his taxes! News media entertainment is hustling us all, and serving us the news in the format and content they want us to react to.

Even the radio airwaves are controlled by these huge entertainment hustlers. When you listen to radio, 80% of the station's playlists match one another. And here's an interesting fact, the popular song *Mrs. Robinson* performed by Simon and Garfunkel has played 6 million times since its release 32 years ago. That equals 32 years of non-stop back to back airplay of one song. I'd like to know who the copyright owner of that song is because they are certainly rich.

These six major hustlers generated box office sales of 7 billion dollars in 2010. I'm sure that number has now doubled. That is twice the box office receipts of over 140 movie studios that made and distributed movies as well. They absolutely show us that conflict of interest is not even a topic of discussion for them by owning both movie studios and news outlets at the same time. Control over the minds of the masses is the agenda, and I must say The Big Hustle is working very well.

AOL, one of the first internet hustlers and now a media giant, spent $124 billion to purchase Time Warner in 2001. That's six times what our U.S. Congress funded to rebuild Iraq. Here's a list of the six major hustler corporations in America and their holdings. If you take your time and put the pieces together properly, you'll slowly begin to realize that these company's agendas, belief systems and principles are always being dictated not by who or what they are, but by who actually owns them.

- **General Electric** owns Comcast, NBC, Universal Pictures, and Focus Pictures

- **News Corp** owns Fox, The Wall Street Journal, and The New York Post

- **Disney** owns ABC, ESPN, Pixar, Miramax, and Marvel Studios

- **Viacom** owns MTV, Nick Jr, BET, CMT

- **Time Warner** owns HBO, TIME, and Warner Brothers

- **CBS** owns Showtime, The Smithsonian Channel, NFL.com, Jeopardy, and 60 Minutes

After all this I'm supposed to believe that these corporate hustlers have an interest in me, my children, impoverished communities and social injustices in and across the country? I'm not buying it! Having major hustlers police you and themselves is not the antidote for change. These massive corporate hustlers manipulate, control and dominate the media landscape of America, and quite possibly the world.

They control ideas from creation to final distribution. Because the internet has become so relevant and a part of their agenda, they have made access to high speed internet a basic public necessity like water and electricity. The giant internet hustlers Facebook and Google are now in the same game. Slowly they are reconstituting the internet in new directions to match the agenda of the six major corporate hustlers. They are trying to steer us to marketers who benefit from mining our personal information. They position products, goods and services to make us believe we want or need it. They are controlling our minds and profiting heavily from it. Our job is to avoid becoming participants in their big hustle.

CELEBRITIES

How is it as a society we've allowed celebrities in the entertainment business to give us advice and direction on our belief systems, politics, products we buy, rearing our children, and to determine by their standards what is right or wrong? We have watched many celebrities go down in flames and yet we still idolize them, and hold onto their philosophies and opinions as if what happened to them was not their fault.

Please hear me out - in no way am I saying that all celebrities are this way and that we shouldn't care about them, their ideas or points of view. But I am saying look at the fruit they produce, period. Have you heard of the saying that you can tell a tree by the fruit it bears? Well you can tell who someone is by how they behave, interact and what they share with the world. I'm sure there are some amazing people who happen to be celebrities, and have stepped up to the plate to show character that is worthy of being modeled after, but it's a small number I assure you.

Are we really that ignorant or have we just given up on making decisions for ourselves? For decades, the entertainment business has used celebrities to change our perspectives on key issues from politics to education, and other subject matters of their choosing. I'm not telling anyone to disregard a person's advice that might make sense to you. Again, I'm saying look at the *walk* not the talk, and who that person is outside of what they might paid to endorse, promote and share.

Over the years, I've watched celebrities tell us not to do something and then walk right out of the door and do the polar opposite of what they told you to do (or not to do). Simple things that used to have so much value has no value at all today. Virtue, morality, character, and honesty has almost become extinct. The media floods us daily with lifestyles of rich and famous teasing us with a desire to want that lifestyle. We watch and duplicate what they do, and want to eat what they eat, drive what they drive, wear what they wear, and raising our children to be just like theirs. Essentially, we've begun to worship what they worship - fame, money and power.

We are being manipulated and controlled at a pace so fast we don't realize it. Celebrities have that power if we allow it. This is just a Big Hustle. It's a drug and the celebrities are the drug dealers. Often the lifestyles of rich and famous people have ended in disaster like bankruptcy, drug abuse and even tragically their untimely death. So why are we following disaster? How are we allowing people who have no standards to establish standards for us?

This is what we've become attracted to. We are following empty images only to find that celebrities are prone to ordinary temptations as we all are. Just like us, they've fallen

for the big hustle but on another level. Fame and celebrity is a

complicated thing to earn and handle, but the enslavement of

those hustled and trying to escape would be difficult for

anyone to handle.

ATHLETES

America is obsessed with professional sports, especially football. I've played golf with at least 25 guys who have been inducted into the NFL Hall of Fame. I've heard countless stories over the years about their lives, their fame and their fans. Because of the open access to their lives via the internet, social media and television, we think we know them personally. We follow the lifestyles of athletes just like we follow the lifestyles of celebrities and other entertainers. Some of these athletes are even bigger than top celebrities.

Whether we like it or not these people have become role models and examples for the young people in this generation. Video games, toys, apparel, and even electronic devices are advertised by some of the world's most notable athletes, and sales numbers are through the roof. Look at the sales of college and professional team jerseys alone. Nike raked in 2.5 billion in sales in 2013, more than any other sports item in the market. Once again football, one of the most violent sports, gets promoted more than other sport in the U.S. with sales that reflect our response to that violence.

Can you see the connection here? You might not see it, but it's The Big Hustle happening here too. Gone are the days when you asked children what they wanted to be and you would often hear one of three choices: policeman, fireman or doctor. I'm not saying that any of these newfound professions are bad choices to strive to do for a living. But I am saying that everything we do is attached to a system that has an agenda, and you may want to know what system these people are controlled by. You might find that how athletes operate in this business is about what they *must* do versus what they would choose to do. Choice goes out the window when represented by a system under the entertainment umbrella.

Pro Sports in America and the entertainment business are joined at the hips. Here's the hustle: the entertainment business is the supplier, the athletes are the drug dealers, and of course we are the junkies hooked on this drug called sports entertainment.

This hustling system uses athletes to build a brand and make money, and oftentimes with college sports, provides little or no compensation for the entertainment those athletes provide and the sacrifices they make. Colleges make millions of dollars from advertising and televising athletic events with the participants, the college athletes, showcasing their talents to make the event successful and the business profitable. These athletes, the stars of the show, received no tangible or monetary compensation at all, but they help generate a substantial amount of revenue. That is nothing but modern day slavery disguised as sports scholarships. What a farce! Shame on these colleges for allowing this to taint the education process, and for participating in the same entertainment hustle philosophy by using these athletes for their own purpose. Greed has made collegiate sports and universities pimp out our young talented adults. I thought college was for promoting education with only professors, deans, and coaches on the payroll. Student athletes should be added to the payroll as well.

The entertainment machine must eat and somebody's got to feed it. Or should I say it has to eat off something or someone? Hopefully one day someone in a position of power and authority can step up to the plate with this issue on behalf of the student athlete who works hard like an employee sacrificing their time and talents for someone else's entertainment and profit.

MANAGERS

It's hard to define what an Entertainment Manager really does. I've been involved in and connected with the entertainment management business for over 25 years and I still can't give you an accurate job description of what we do because we do everything, anything and sometimes nothing at all. Some managers grew up with their clients as childhood friends. Or you have the family member manager who may not be the best person for the job but you feel like you can trust them to have your best interests at heart. Or you have an associate or friend who from the beginning looks super shady, but you think you need a shady person on your side to deal with the shady people in this business.

Then there are managers like myself who truly have your best interests first – will help watch your finances, never steal from you, always fighting the establishment, takes care of you when you're broke and down on your luck, suffers through all the tough times, and thinks it's an honor to work with you. Of course, that's the person the artist screws over when they hit the big time. Unless you control everything for the artist the odds are not in your favor.

Here's an analogy of how screwed up the management side is. When it comes to management it's about as safe as throwing dice in Las Vegas. You may hit 7 or 11, you may get a point and make it, you may get a point and hold it for a while and then throw 7, and then you may just hit craps, 2, 3 or 12. But here is something you should know: the games in Las Vegas are fixed. They aren't designed for you to win, only to entertain you.

Years ago, I managed a five-member music group called *Cold Premiere* that could sing and perform as good as any group at the time. A friend introduced me to this group from

Ohio. I went out to Ohio to meet them and see if they were interested in moving to Los Angeles to pursue their dream of securing a major recording contract. I invested a good amount of up front capital on them. I paid for everything from rent, their parent's utility bills and the group's relocation expenses. It hurts to even mention it because I'm trying very hard to still love these gentlemen today.

I had a lot of music industry contacts so I set up a showcase for them and invited record labels to watch them perform at the hottest club in the country at that time, Paradise 24 in Los Angeles. All the A-list stars like Prince, Magic Johnson, Eddie Murphy, Madonna, Sylvester Stallone, Jim Brown, LA Reid and Babyface, Jimmy Jam and Terry Lewis, Arsenio Hall, Paula Abdul, and anybody else who was a celebrity in Los Angeles at the time frequented this nightclub.

The night they were to perform was the same night MC Hammer showed up to perform and of course, he killed it. My guys were scared to death but they knew they were good, and I knew the fear would go away when they hit the stage. When MC Hammer left the stage the crowd was screaming Go Hammer! Go Hammer! Then my guys came out, the music came on, and they began their performance. It took a minute for the crowd to reset after MC Hammer, but as the guys continued their show, the audience responded and everyone in the place went bananas by the time the song was over.

The energy in that club was palpable. They were on a high. When the show ended, multiple people approached them asking where they're from and if they were they signed to a label. Anyone who was there that night remembers that group. An executive from Giant Records whom I knew through a friend came to me and said she wanted to sign Cold Premiere right away, and wanted to discuss the details in the morning. I wanted to believe her, but I've heard that line so many times in LA, but I agreed to talk the following day.

Well the unthinkable happened. Giant Records actually called, and within 3 weeks we were starting to sign contracts for a deal with a major record label. Giant was one of the newest labels in town with fresh money. They were about to do the movie "New Jack City" starring Wesley Snipes and the soundtrack as well, so I knew for sure my guys would be included on that project. Well I didn't know it at that the time, but that movie project would be a bad omen for my group.

Being an entertainment manager is not easy. One mistake I made was hiring a young lady who quit her job at the IRS to work for me full time and help manage the group, only to find out later she was just a groupie. I don't know why I thought I needed support since I had handled everything just fine up to that point. I gave that woman way too much authority and she abused it, all the while sleeping with one of the group members. That never ends well. Then there was an executive at Giant Records who started trying to manage my group behind my back because she thought I was too soft. Well that's because I wasn't stealing money from the artists, which was something she felt comfortable doing. In addition to combating these influences as their manager, the group had people whispering in their ears trying to get a cut of what was about to happen. These young kids were afraid and didn't know what to do. Nevertheless, I continued to get them as much visibility as I could, including an appearance in a movie called "A Class Act" starring the rap group Kid 'n Play.

With all the confusion going on and working out contract details, the record label, who was the culprit of most of the disaster anyway, signed a new group, Color Me Badd. You might remember their huge hit from the New Jack City soundtrack "I Wanna Sex You Up." I guess my group's songs didn't promote sex enough because after that song's release, my group got put on the back shelf. And that was the end of Cold Premiere's music career. Those guys would never be the same. A couple of them did some other things in the industry but nothing compared to the potential they had to become successful artist.

Here are a few lessons both artists and managers can learn:

- If you manage an artist and they don't live in the city you're doing business in, request that they stay home until it's time to get to work. Being in a city like Los Angeles sitting around waiting on deals to come through or to begin working is not good. Too many distractions and it can be costly for the manager. Also as a side note, when people who work together start sleeping together, it's just a matter of time before the ship begins to sink.

- Never give away your money, service, or information for free to any one, especially if the content is related to what you do for a living. It just never turns out nice.

- Don't ever believe anything an executive at an entertainment company tells you. The majority of them lie through their teeth with a smile on their face. First, they are not in charge, someone higher up always is. Most creative people are pretty fair and just want to be good at their craft, but remember there are snakes on both sides of the fence. Most of us would never think so, but artistic people can be just as much of a snake as an executive or manager. The worst part about the artist as the snake is they walk away playing the victim and become part of the big hustle as well.

Even though that story sounds unfair to myself as a manager, there is a still another side of management, a darker side that relates more to what this book is about. It amazes me how the entertainment industry is not accountable for those who are taken advantage of on both sides, manager and artist. People are allowed to rob, cheat, steal and leave a person who has rightfully earned their money at a financial disadvantage, often in debt and with tax problems.

Entertainment is one business that has the ability, know how, influence and power to structure a program to protect artists from being used and abused. They could regulate percentages paid to managers. They could have an oversight division to enforce penalties on those who steal and manipulate artists. Sadly, they won't do a thing about it because people who steal, hurt and cause harm will always get a pass in the entertainment business.

Never forget - it's all The Big Hustle. It seems that artists in entertainment are taken advantage of more than anyone else across other businesses. Here are some extreme examples to assess the validity of the statements I've made. The first example of a major artist being taken advantage of is the life and career of Elvis Presley. People often talk about how much of a musical genius he was, and in doing so they always forget to mention his manager. Colonel Tom Parker did a deal with Elvis to receive 50% of his *before* tax income. I may be crazy but that seems high, unless Elvis is not telling us something about his relationship with his manager. In my experience, that's an absurdly high percentage to pay someone to manage you. Whether I like Elvis' music, movies or him personally has nothing to do with this. I believe that any system that allows people to be taken advantage of without industry regulation and without bringing attention to it is just wrong.

How about Frank Weber, Billy Joel's manager who was accused of stealing $30 million before tax dollars from him. He also was his brother in law and the godfather of his daughter. What a shame! This business turns people you think you know and trust into your worst nightmare.

This is why the theme of entertainment is betrayal of trust. Lying, stealing, cheating, and doing things that harm those who have entrusted you with their entire lives is not only condoned, it gets rewarded! People who do this underhanded, backstabbing heartless work are given the best deals, kickbacks, and put in positions of higher authority at major entertainment companies, continuing that same behavior. I've been known to say that the entertainment business is the only business where you fail upward with promotion.

I assure you that the people who do this to others are hurting within themselves, because people in pain are the ones who inflict hurt the most. In a way, they are victims who became perpetrators.

The only way to curb this activity is to never trust anyone with your money, and never give someone the opportunity to be tempted to steal from you because trust me, most will. Money and management go well together when in small amounts, but as the money grows so does the temptation. I'm sure that at least 90% percent of the people on this planet have never seen a million dollars cash in their lives and if they do, something in them may change how they see money. Trust me I've seen its effect on people time and time again. *The love of money is the root of all evil* is a true statement when you have access to large amounts of money. It enchants people, driving them to want to have it – or take it.

Management relationships start off similar to marriages because that's really what they are, a union between two people or entities. Like everything we desire in life, it starts off beautiful, and then somewhere down the line things change, you grow apart and go in a different direction. Often that is dictated by the lifestyles of the people involved. Drug use, drug dealers, alcohol abuse, personal relationships, creativity, family, friends, entertainment companies, attorneys, business managers, and others begin to put pressure on that relationship. This leads people who don't have the capacity for pressure to explode, and fear sets in. When that happens, people resort to becoming selfish and only think about themselves. At that point the management part of the relationship, which is surely in a tailspin by now, is over. The key to a successful artist/manager relationship is respect and fear of penalty, period. It's not trust or chemistry like most people think, and it's not education, experience or how many people you know in the entertainment business, although those can be important factors. It simply comes down to individual respect and fear of getting caught.

Outside of the entertainment industry, if you steal from your client, you would certainly be going to jail. It's called embezzlement. To be clear, the definition of embezzlement is the theft or misappropriation of funds placed in one's trust or belonging to one's employer. As an entertainment manager, you are likely entrusted with funds to manage that are not yours. In the law books, embezzlement is a class b felony if the property is valued at $25,000 dollars or more. punishable by 5 to 20 years in prison and a fine up to $15,000 dollars. The sentencing judge can also require restitution. Fear of penalty and prosecution is the only way people will respect the artist's money.

If you are considering working with a manager for any reason, here are some things to ask and consider:

- Their management history
- What other jobs have they had that require confidentiality or trust in money matters

- Their criminal background record

- Their credit score

- Who is in their social circle

- Relationship with their family - all of them

- Educational background

- Entertainment work history

- Special projects they've created or worked on

- Talk to people who know them well (character references)

- Exactly what you want them to do for you and for how long

- Establish a contractual agreement that you can get out of, and is fair to the other party as well

Most importantly, write an incentive agreement. If your manager performs well, they are paid well. If not, the compensation reflects that. Like anything else in life, why should your hard work as the artist and the lack of theirs

reward them and penalize you?

THE ARTIST

The word *artist* is a broad term to describe a creative person in entertainment but can be applied to any person who sells, promotes trades, or in some cases prostitutes their creative talents or gifts for money, fame, or power. The artist is the person most taken advantage of because they are the creators of the product we all buy, sell and consume. So at times, the artist can become everybody's big hustle.

As I said before, to understand the relationship entertainment has with an artist, you must understand the dynamics of how one pimps a prostitute. The pimp convinces her that he is her savior, and that he has what no one else can give her. It all comes easy for the pimp because most of the time the prostitute *chooses* her pimp. There's a saying I used to hear on the streets when pimps would talk about the process of how they get women. They would say *women do the picking and choosing, and pimps do the hiring, firing and suspending*. Sound familiar? Well it is, this is the same mantra of the entertainment business. Always has been and always will be.

Here's how it works. The artist/prostitute always believes the pimp will be her guide and protector, and makes her believe that by following him people will esteem her. All the things life has denied her for whatever reason is now within reach. He lets her know that there are other pimps out there who are not as nice, and he wants to protect her. He assures her that he can take her life to a level she can only dream of.

She begins to trust him, she shares with him all her secrets, hurts, pains and vulnerabilities, but he makes sure he never exposes *his* vulnerabilities because it could harm the agenda of the relationship.

She comes from abuse of all kinds, sexual, mental, emotional, abandonment, and often physical, so the haven he offers her in him sounds like a great escape. She decides she wants to be on his team. She's so excited to be part of what she thinks is a family she'll do anything, compromise her values, morals, integrity, and betray those who have been true to her all for her new savior, the pimp.

And so, she leaves a life of dysfunction for a deeper level of dysfunction disguised as a safety net for all of life's issues. She begins to repeat one of the most naive things that I hear creative people say all the time, *I love this so much I would do it for free*. Trust me, that was already the plan so welcome aboard. Taking advantage of people through bribery, extortion, manipulation, and outright lying is just a normal day in entertainment.

All businesses have some form of these dealings going on but not to the degree of how it's done in entertainment. Over the years, I've advised artists and creative people to be very careful with whom you do business with. Find out their agenda, because the same people that are making things happen for you will be the same people taking it away from you.

I caution artists to beware of being taken advantage of because in entertainment they're at the front door, back door and at every window. There are tons of stories about the relationships between artists and entertainment companies. Most of them don't end in favor the artist.

I don't have the fascination over artists as celebrities that I had back when I first got into this business because I've met, worked with, and socialized with so many high-profile people since then that is has sort of worn off. I still love what artists do and I admire their amazing ability to create. I also realize who they are and what they are always up against, and I would never want to be in their shoes. Because of this, my compassion is toward the artist versus entertainment companies. I've done everything imaginable for artists over the years. I've taken them to rehab, and have gone into drug houses to retrieve them. I've helped them read over difficult contracts, helped them realize someone was stealing their money, given them a place to live, bought cars for them, taken money out of my pocket to give them, taken care of their children and other family members, cooked meals, and to the best of my ability stayed true to an allegiance of confidentiality about their personal business.

Artists should be revered for the talents God has bestowed on them, but instead the framework of this industry is built on a design that hustles talent, and can pimp out an artist until they are worthless. It's hard to know who to trust when everyone wants a piece of the pie. I've come across very few managers, attorneys, and entertainment companies that have gone to the lengths that I have for the artists I've worked for and with. In this business, the artist must equip themselves with the knowledge to make sound decisions on whom they offer a piece of their pie to. If not, the artist can easily destroy himself by making the wrong choices.

THE ATTORNEYS

There's only one way to describe attorneys in entertainment: The Good, The Bad and The Ugly. Forrest Gump said it best when he said ...*It's like a box of chocolates, you never know what you're gonna get.* That's been my entertainment experience with attorneys. If you've only had great experiences with attorneys in this business, either you're an attorney yourself or you're doing what a lot of attorneys are good at – lying.

One of the challenges attorneys face most is what is determined to be ethical, and by what and who's standards. In entertainment, this line is not well defined. Even those who may have written the rules for ethics had to consider something called conflict of interest, meaning what's good for the client is often opposite of what's good for the attorney. It's a tough call but attorneys, regardless of what we think of them, are human first.

Regardless of what an attorney charges you, they make their money by providing a service for you, and the more things you need them for and ask of them, the more money they make. This is where the deception and temptation comes in, where the attorney begins to make the client believe there's more services, protection and consultation needed from him/her than there truly is.

In order to make himself feel better about the guilt of his actions, the attorney begins to lie, not only to the client but to himself. In his mind, he resolves it by creating excuses that certain facts are more important than others, therefore overestimating the work and billable time. This may sound like a big hustle because it is. That's what attorneys are, hustlers!

I'm sure if you looked hard enough you could find a few attorneys in this business who are representing their clients in an ethical manner but I assure you you're going to have to look very hard.

The biggest conflict I've found with attorneys in the entertainment business is they are generally on both sides. Normally when a person plays on both sides, the one who usually wins is the one with the most money and/or power. Who's right or wrong has nothing to do with the outcome.

Always remember an attorney has 4 obligations to himself upon meeting you:

- Maintain confidentiality

- Advocate for your best interest with a certain amount of zeal

- Conduct themselves as keepers of the law which they are admitted to practice

- Charge a reasonable and fair amount of money for the services rendered to you

Yet somehow during the course of your attorney and client relationship, the understanding and order of these standards either get compromised, removed, or prioritized in the order of what's important to the attorney, putting his needs over yours.

As earlier stated, the responsibility we have in choosing an attorney(s) is to find out which side they are really on. I've realized that most attorneys in entertainment know each other very well, more than they want to admit Many of them went to school together, play golf together, their children attend the same schools, and sometimes the spouse is working for a competing firm.

One of the ways to attempt to protect yourself from this form of nepotism is to only allow that attorney to perform services in their specialized area. Entertainment attorneys specialize in creating contracts, handling copyright, protecting writers and creators against infringement, acquiring the rights to literary properties, negotiating deals for options, collaboration agreements, script submissions, work for hire agreements, non-disclosure agreements, and any other aspects of entertainment business. Your entertainment attorney should never advise or counsel you on family matters, criminal matters, real estate matters, or on any issue outside of entertainment business. Find another attorney that specializes in those other areas if needed. If your entertainment attorney advises you otherwise, that's your red flag to find another attorney. You have the authority to hold them accountable and keep them in their lane.

Avoid dealing with unethical and incompetent attorneys by educating yourself on their business and what they are paid to do. Remember, they protecting a process using legalities but they work for you. Don't forget it's always a big hustle.

AGENTS

Agents are the individuals responsible to keep you working once you are in the business, but not a day before. They assist management and/or the artist in finding work with major entertainment companies, production companies, and they themselves will package film and television projects for their clients.

I don't know how the role of an agent came to be, but I believe that years ago companies realized that since the artist has a representative (managers), that they should have an individual to manage their interests. And voila - the role of an agent was born. I've always viewed agents as personal managers for entertainment companies, but they are a different kind of manager. One main difference is that an agent must be licensed by the state whereas managers do not require professional licensure. This is why you'll see many artists managed by friends, family and just about anyone who looks the part. I assure you some of the theft that happens at the hands of the artists' managers would decrease significantly with professional licensure and government regulation.

If we're being honest, Agents work for companies and not for you. It's important that you do not forget this. Agents represent actors, film directors, screenwriters, performers, musicians, artist, professional athletes, and broadcast journalists. They are supposed to be the mediator between the talent and those who employ the talent. In terms of compensation, agents are usually paid 10% of the artist's income and managers generally get 15% and up to as much as 50%. Legitimate agents and managers never ask for up-front money from their clients. They work strictly on a commission basis only. The job and duties of a talent agent involves tons of communication and negotiation making phone calls, selling their clients (the talent) and occasionally wining and dining prospective employers for their clients. Because technology has been rapidly advancing, talent agents handle a lot of their duties and responsibilities online, but it still takes face to face meetings with clients and employers to finalize deals.

The top cities for major talent agents are Los Angeles, New York, and Nashville, although there are some boutique agencies with agents as well. At the end of the day, agents are just as much a part of the hustle as everyone else. As expected in this business, their loyalty goes to the highest bidder, which is usually the major entertainment companies. For the artist, it's another opportunity to be hustled by the industry.

PROTECT AGAINST THE BIG HUSTLE

Not everyone in this business will lie, cheat, and steal but I do believe that anyone can lie, cheat and steal under the right circumstances. Unfortunately, the situation presents itself more often in this business than others.

My philosophy when working with others on money matters is to always go into the situation assuming they will take advantage of you. Then you will do always take precaution steps to protect yourself and your money Always remember that the people who handle your affairs work *for* you, not *with* you. They must go through the same process as any employee who handles money, legal documents, etc.

Those skilled at taking advantage of others will know everything about you, your background, weaknesses and finances. They know you are inexperienced at this game. They do their homework so you should do yours. The first suggestion to protect yourself in legal partnerships is a simple one - Google. In this modern age of technology, you can find out any and everything online if you dig deep enough. Do a detailed key word search (called Boolean search) of the name, aliases and states/city of employ or residence, and other relevant business terms to improve search results. Also, consider conducting a legitimate criminal background check of the states the individual has lived and worked in. If you haven't learned a thing from this book and still want to hire someone without taking precautional steps, DO NOT let them handle your money. Period.

One of the more serious dangers of the grave mishandling of finances is IRS issues. Can you imagine, someone steals your money and *you* end up paying taxes on that stolen money? Sadly, it does happen. You want to build a system of basic checks and balances to protect yourself. There's no guarantees but these steps should expose misdealings before they become more grievous offenses. I've outlined protective measures I recommend:

- Never under any circumstances allow anyone to sign checks, withdraw money, or have Power of Attorney over any account. That includes your parents, family members, coaches, friends and your homie who you grew up with. Power of Attorney means you've given them permission to be you and act as your representative (without your knowledge or approval). Even if you have only a basic understanding of math and finances, trust me you'll be just fine. You're better off making your own mistakes with money versus what someone else will do with that power.

- If you must give someone a bank credit cards/debit cards/store cards/gas cards, make sure that the limit on those cards does not exceed $1,500. If more is needed, let them come to you to ask for it in cash or check form, preferably in writing (email, text, etc.). This is how you establish a documented money trail. If you are dealing with honest people, they will never have a problem with this arrangement.

- Don't trust someone's word. Verify everything and always request receipts and duplicate copies.

- Make sure the people who work for you do NOT have relationships/friendships with the people who work at your bank and other financial institutions. If someone recommends a bank/financial institution to you to use, ask why they gave the recommendation. If they know someone who works, steer clear.

- Check on your money every day. Make this a quick ritual every morning over breakfast. It doesn't take much time. It takes at least a couple days for someone to withdraw and steal any significant amount of money so if you check it daily, you'll notice it.

- If and when you have the resources to do so, don't inform anyone but hire an individual to review the work and watch what other people are doing for you. Often times employees conspire together to steal from you. If someone they don't know is watching it will be easy to catch.

- As you are getting established and start making money, make sure most of your liquid money is protected in government-backed institutions. They have been proven over time to be the most reliable source of investment and savings. You can invest in other ways like real estate later on when you are fully established financially to take on those riskier investments.

- Always keep a certain amount of cash stored somewhere that nobody but you and God know where it is. And don't ask anyone to retrieve. Don't be lazy – get it yourself.

- When the time is right, learn about investing in real estate. If done properly it's one of the greatest investments you could ever make. When you are ready, go to an established and reputable real estate company versus your friend's friend who happens to do some real estate on the side.

- One thing that wealthy people have known for years but don't talk about is that insurance is a money maker, especially life insurance. There's a significant tax advantage to it and there's a sure bet that everyone will die at some point. This makes life insurance a good investment to explore.

- Owning a residence, if you have the resources to do so, is always better than renting or leasing. Renting, regardless of what anyone says is a liability.

- Don't spend more than you need to. There's nothing wrong with negotiating a price/deal. It also allows you to be patient in the buying process, and over time you may feel later that you don't even want what you thought you did.

- Establish a reasonable spending pattern and don't exceed it even if your income rises. When you're on a spending pattern, it allows you to be safe in the lean times and save more in the good times. This business has no guarantees.

- Live within your means. Showing off what you have means nothing to anyone (except those that want to take it from you!). People who like to flaunt what they have usually do so to compensate for something that's missing inside. Dress conservative and be conservative regardless of how much you truly do have.

- Remember when you have money, financial institutions want you in debt for life. This keeps you a slave to a system that cares nothing about you. The best way to build wealth is to learn to spend less. A great example is one of the richest men in the world, Warren Buffett, and his habits on frugal living/spending. Statistics aren't always correct but they say the average 35-year-old person in this generation will die in debt. Don't borrow more than you need.

- Learn to listen and learn from others. Just because you do a little research online doesn't mean you're smart. Wisdom can't be bought, it comes from trials, tribulations and life experiences. The good book says

"Is not wisdom found among the aged? Does not long life bring understanding?" Job 12:12 NIV. You would be a fool not to learn from those that have accomplished that which you want to achieve.

MY FINAL THOUGHTS

When I think of an example of a well-known artist you may have witnessed being hustled by this business, Dave Chappelle immediately comes to mind. This standup comedian, writer, actor, and producer who I believe is one of the greatest comedic minds ever basically said this to industry moguls when he walked away from their $50M+ deal - he'll be a prostitute but on his own terms.

I say that because he is still working in the business today doing stand-up and deals with Netflix. According to the philosophy of this business, he's still in the same place he was before he walked away, but just working for a different pimp. At the end of the day it's still all a big hustle. You can't get out of their web. If you enjoy entertainment, want to be in entertainment, work for anyone in entertainment, or just want to quit the grind of trying to break in the biz and go back home to watch a little TV, you're caught up in the entertainment web.

The entertainment business will continue to manipulate and control our children, our minds, and be a detriment to the fabric of our society. I don't see light at the end of this dark and scary tunnel.

Daily we stay glued to our cell phones or TV screen that tells us what to do, when to do it, and how to do it. Our children are being taken into a world of interactive fantasy. Entertainment is our drug and we are addicted consumers. And there are so many ways to get high. We have unlimited 24/7 access to our drug via phones, computers, tablets, television, and smartwatches; at home, restaurants, bars, schools, sporting events, airports, cars and even churches. Every. Place. You. Go. That's not freedom, that's restrictive liberty.

Then you have the drug dealers waiting in line to push their drug and agenda: comedy, music, the news media, politicians and even religion, all taking a shot at selling us their drug, following the lead from their supplier...the entertainment business.

I'm on this drug as well but I'm in rehab. As a society, we've fallen and I don't believe we're going to get up from this one. All we can do is protect our hearts and minds from this super seductive juggernaut that may very well eventually control everything we do, see, touch, taste, and smell.

A Netflix executive once made a joke saying in 20 or 50 years we will be taking a personalized blue pill that will allow you to hallucinate in the way you want to be entertained (get high), and a white pill that brings you back to normality. This business wants the future of entertainment to be pharmacological. That is scary. But there are some things technology just can't do, and that is where we should invest our time and energy; by showing love, spending quality time with people we care about, being helpful and showing kindness as human beings, and taking care of our mind and bodies for as long as we walk this earth. And as parents, this is your responsibility to your children and the next generation. Remember that we are not machines or what any organized system tells us that we are. We are not programmable. We are human beings with a choice to control or be controlled. God has given us all free will and we should use it.

The expression of artistic creativity must continue, but with caution for how you monetize your worth and allow yourself to become capitalized for profit when you want to share that talent with the world. God gave us all talents and we should want to use them for good, particularly if we want to continue to experience a world worth living in.

James Arceneaux

Made in the USA
San Bernardino, CA
11 February 2018